GUNS
and
GUTS

GUNS *and* GUTS

The Courage to Act

Carla R. Mancari

Celestial Literary Group

To
The courageous among us

Guns and Guts: The Courage To Act

Copyright 2018, Carla R. Mancari. *Guns and Guts: The Courage to Act,* revision, all rights reserved. No part of this book may be reproduced or transmitted in any form or by any means without the author's written permission. Revised 5/15/2023.

The contents of this book are not meant to take the place of qualified medical professionals or therapists. There is no expressed or implied guarantee regarding the effects of the suggestions or the liability taken.

CONTENTS

Acknowledgments
Preface

1. The Rise of The Courageous
   Standing Up 11

2. Courage
   Being Brave 16

3. Tug of War
   Standing Firm 19

4. Doubts and Temptations
   Distractions 26

5. Change
   Conversion 30

6. A Mind Change
   Through the Heart 33

7. Choices and Decisions
   Selection and Carry Through 38

8. Emotions
   Rising Energy 43

9 Accept, Allow, and Respect
An Atmosphere of Peace 57

10 Dedication
Discouraged and Tested 60

11. Hugs
God's Embrace 64

12. Topic Tips
Practical Guidance 68

13. Spiritual Heart Center
Pure Energy 72

14. The Minute Meditation 75

15. Mini-Exercises 83
Helpers

16. Maintenance and Balance
A Strong Positive Force 90

Author 93

Author's Books 95

Notes 111

ACKNOWLEDGMENTS

I appreciate all of the young people and their supporters for having the courage to make a difference during difficult times.

A heartfelt thanks to Mary Carpenter for reviewing and editing the manuscript. This work could not have been accomplished without her dedication.

I am grateful for the Minute Meditation. It's a revelation without which this work would not be possible.

PREFACE

Guns and Guts: The Courage to Act was inspired by the young peoples' movement "Never Again" and the "March for Our Lives." The very young and teenagers' display of love and guts to rise and take on the politicians and the NRA emphasizes courage of the highest order. *Guns and Guts: The Courage to Act* is a contribution to the young people's profound, elevated, and far-reaching actions to be involved in saving lives. There are many traps and snares that await you. It will require your on-going courage to act.

This book offers you support and tools that may be used to shore up your resolve. A review of the Spiritual Heart Center, the Minute Meditation, and the Mini-Exercises are included. The Minute Meditation may assist you in continuing your journey for gun reform and beyond.

All are presented to help support brave young soldier civilians on their inner and outer journey of change. It is hoped that what is written here will help prepare and sustain you for the encounters along your inner and outer journey for gun and heart changes. "You, your, and yours" is always used in the plural.

ONE

THE RISE OF THE COURAGEOUS
Standing Up

I never expected it to happen in my lifetime, but here it is. It has taken the very young and teenagers to have the guts to stand up to the NRA, to stand up and to say, "Enough, no more, and never again." Adults have not had the guts to do it. The politicians make excuses, but do not have one good reason for their fear of the NRA.

You, young people, are courageous taking on the gun lobby with guts and tenacity never before seen. You are young solder civilians at war for our country because of the many who have abandoned their moral values. You youth are showing us the way, what it takes. Sure, you will have strong opposition, but you have guts on your side, something that many politicians and adults sadly lack.

Reflections

Abraham Lincoln, Gandhi, and Mother Teresa, each was a power of one who made a difference in the lives of many. They were each one an individual who cared about the whole of humankind. They cared enough to do something.

And how about Oprah or Bill Gates? They care enough to make a difference in the lives of many. You young teenagers are the same. You are a power of one who can see what is happening to the lives and the health of the children. You are a power of one who can start with yourselves and ultimately make a difference.

The media of the United States offer comprehensive data on school killings and health-related issues. Unfortunately, the news consists of a bit of good and a lot of bad. Media exposure is not getting the message through. Let's face it: fear, threats, hell, and damnation sermons are not very popular or practical anymore. Anyway, they have been tried and retried. You can only take so much bad news before you dim your sights, close your ears, and shut down.

It's easier to turn away from bad news, especially when the topic is about the perils of guns. Short of someone setting your hair on fire, it is becoming more difficult to get the message of gun reform across. The quickest way to turn individuals off is to repeat the endless warning statistics and catastrophic predictions. If they had ever worked, change for gun reform would not be withering away.

Lives are lost from thoughtless disregard for the necessity of gun reform. From where is the much-needed help going to come? Can technology help? Can *God* help? God didn't create the mess that the politicians and the NRA have created.

Waiting for an opportunity, the right moment, or others to act first is a waste of time. Waiting creates an imaginary future holding pattern. Whenever you are waiting for others to act, you are in a dead zone, a mental freeze. It is better to accept, allow, and respect the choices and decisions others make for themselves so you can get on with the work that *begins with you.*

The gun environment is in intensive care. It's fighting for its life, *your* lives. When the death and near death of the children is obvious, it is time to acknowledge that the children need you *and* your need depends on each other.

In your young lives, realize that you were successful. The moment you were willing to stand up and take action, you were successful. Failure follows inaction.

TWO

COURAGE
Being Brave

You might think courage (being brave) is not necessary for you young teenagers to stand up against overwhelming odds. However, it is. And it will take courage for you also to maintain your dedication to a mighty cause. At the beginning of your journey for gun reform, your actions are vested with courage. There will be many times you will be challenged. There is always the force of others and situations to distract you from your intent.

When you are being tested, will you continue to be courageous? Will you, with unflinching courage, surrender your cause to no one? It takes courage for you to journey from the relative known of your daily young lives to the reality of the political world. It will require courage for you to accept the setbacks, the push backs, and belittlements of your character.

Stepping out of your comfort zone and holding fast to your beliefs may require courage of the highest order. Living out from your truth takes courage never before known. To do otherwise is to insult your integrity.

It takes courage for you to say, "Yes" to a cause that many politicians are willing to lose their souls over. Your path is a minefield of hate and ignorance from many. Have courage, stay the course. Yes, it does take courage, but you possess it. You believe in your cause.

THREE

TUG OF WAR
Standing Firm

There may be many times during your gut-wrenching tug of war that you must rely on your belief in your cause to continue. Standing firm in your belief during a difficult process of changing hearts and minds may require all of the inner strength that you can muster. You may come to realize that life tends to change, and those around you are not always receptive to change. It may take sheer willpower to continue down a path of change when there are others who cannot bend and are not flexible.

You are no longer a sleepwalker caught up in your teenage pursuits. Once you have stepped up to the plate, you are held accountable to finish the race and to weather the storms that may befall you. Your saving Grace is to remember that the children need you. To argue that they do not is an exercise in futility. But, of course, they need you. Who else do they have?

The children need every "you" it can get, but let's start with you. Doesn't everyone want to be needed by someone or something? Look no further. You are in the right place at the right time.

True Story:

A huge, naked, fat, crazy man stands on a corner and spits on individuals as they pass by. The locals consider him the town's fool. So they do their best to ignore him.

One day a rickshaw driver passes by, and the crazy man spits on him. The rickshaw driver has his most profitable day ever. He tells his other fellow rickshaw drivers that he believes his good luck is because he had been spit on that morning by the crazy fool. Sure enough, rickshaw drivers are lining up the following morning to be spit on. The moral of this story: the bigger the fool, the bigger the following.

~~

Some politicians are willing to follow a fool. Obedience to individual/s who would cause harm to our children for their political sake is blind obedience, which has no purpose. You are wiser than your elders who would give blind obedience to a fool.

Things have a way of changing when your emotions rise in defense of gun reform. Deciding that the children need *you* requires only one prerequisite—"now." "Is my life and the lives of the children important now? Will I contribute to the welfare of myself and others now?"

You are always in the now, and it is now that you are being asked to decide. Tomorrow's now may require a change, but today's now, requires a decision. You have made it.

The priority placed on meeting the need for gun reform makes a difference in your lives and the lives of your family and friends. It is not outer pressure that makes you realize the need for gun reform. It all comes from your inner passion for doing the right thing at the right time.

Time and effort are wasted on the notion, "Should I or shouldn't I? "Is the need for gun reform real or not?" You are doing what is necessary. All of the "ifs" and "buts" are escape hatches that are used to avoid committing.

"Ifs and buts" may be the most frequent responses heard from fools when they are faced with an invitation to step up and be accounted for in the cause to help the children. Ifs are always predicated on conditions, and buts seek a backdoor out. They both say, "I am not ready. I am not willing. I am not prepared. I will not take the time or make an effort to help."

Ifs and buts fool no one, including you. They are mind games the politicians play to win the NRA's support ($$$). Whenever you hear politicians using an "if or a but," stop to ask yourself if making excuses and procrastinating not to meet the need for gun reform is worth the lives of the children. There are many ways to procrastinate and put off an opportunity to make a difference. Anything to occupy the minds and time of those caught in the grips of the NRA will do. But, then, there is always the promise, "I will get to it soon, if not now, later, if not today, tomorrow. Let's talk about it, *and* talk about it. Is any subject being talked about, analyzed, or scrutinized more than gun reform? Politicians can always make 101 excuses for putting off the gun reform needed but rarely is there one good reason.

You need only to be aware of the constant school shootings to realize it needs attention. The politicians have many distractions vying for their attention. They pick and choose, and if they continue to choose to neglect gun reform, the children lose. You have an opportunity to give help where a great need for help exists. Don't give up the tug of war for gun reform.

You are special, unique individuals who are capable of doing whatever you decide. Don't shortchange yourselves. No other can step up with your particular gifts, talents, and potential for caring about gun reform.

You have the power to acknowledge that the children need you. Unless you can value and appreciate your place in history now, you will step into the trap of less-deserving things getting your unequivocal attention. The help that gun reform needs lies with you. Your energy knows no weariness and cannot be thwarted. The work you do will be reflected in all you do in your practical daily life.

You are here to make a difference. The children need your support to improve and save their lives. As you depend on the air you breathe, the children depend on you. They need all of the support that they can get from you. Give it. The children need *you*. Don't let them down.

Four

DOUBTS *and* TEMPTATIONS
Distractions

As teenagers, you are prime targets for doubts and temptations. Doubts and temptations will be as attractive as possible and make all the noise necessary to grab your attention away from your goal. Don't be fooled into believing because you are at the moment dedicated to making gun reform; you are immune to doubts and temptations. They will arise.

All around you, there may be doubts and temptations to please others, to take an easier, more familiar way. Unfortunately, there are no more significant obstacles or hindrances to moving forward than the ever-present haunting doubts and temptations. They will come from every direction at the most unexpected times.

Doubts hold hands with temptations. For all practical purposes, the goal is the same, to distract you from the way of rightness that you have chosen. Doubts and temptations require your choice and decision for you to move in their direction. Once you have done so, they attach you to whatever will keep you from staying the course.

Doubts and temptations may trigger a chain reaction leading to wavering, distrust, hesitation, and a lack of creativity. This may slow your forward progress. At times, doubts and temptations may freeze your ability to move forward.

Doubts and temptations will take you down faster than a blow on the head. They may creep in before, during, or after a successful event. On a difficult day, you may have doubts and temptations whether to stop, stay, or go forward.

Doubts and temptations do not have a sense of proportion. There may be doubts and temptations when there doesn't appear any progress, and there are doubts and temptations when there *is* progress. With doubts and temptations, it is always a lose, lose situation.

Doubts and temptations have no respect for bringing about change. They may attack your self-esteem, threaten your sanity, and will do anything to distract you from the path of gun reform that you have chosen. Doubts and temptations are smooth talkers and polite. Be aware; they do not play fair. You should be ever vigilant of the distractions that would take you to a time and space of doubts and temptations.

Doubts and temptations may linger as long as possible. However, obedience and discipline to your cause will stifle the wayward doubts and temptations, unraveling them. Accept all of the honest support you are given and be grateful that you are the chosen soldier civilians to succeed where others have failed.

Five

CHANGE
Conversion

As you progress on a journey for gun reform, change may reveal itself within and outside of your lives. It is a sense of an emotional difference among those who resist gun reform. When you are drawn to seek to do what is necessary, you can be sure a sense of change has begun within you. It can be intentional or unintentional. Whenever you appear or "feel" differently, there is the tendency to refer to the difference as a "change."

Change may be difficult to handle and cause emotional turmoil when relating to others. Whenever you cause a change, you change. As you attempt to adjust to a new way of being, family and old friends may become distant. Describing the change in *your* change may be difficult.

You have chosen to take on an adult responsibility for making gun reform. Therefore, it brings a quickening of maturing. But, for a time, gun reform may cause an inner and outer struggle. The young "selves" with whom you were comfortable, may be slowly (and at times, not so slowly) dying. Allow the young "selves" to go quietly into the night.

Six

A
MIND CHANGE
Through The Heart

There will be many who will attempt to sway you from your chosen goal. There will be times when you will be challenged. Your journey for gun reform may be threatening to other individuals.

Your being grounded in your strong beliefs for gun reform may concern those who stand on shaky ground. Your conviction and certainty of the necessity for reform in gun laws invite a disturbance that causes others to rebel against you. Those who are riddled with doubts are questioning their own position. Even a mind confronted with facts is wasted on a hardened heart.

The only way to changing a mind is through the heart. A hardened heart reflects a closed mind. A heart changed is a mind changed. Do not be disturbed or dismayed by individuals who are neither ready nor prepared to accept gun reform. Their time to do what is necessary, has not come. Rejoice that your time has come.

The politicians and the NRA conjuring up excuses for neglecting this need won't wash. It's always, "If I support gun reform, I would not be protecting the second amendment. I would help, but I must consider the American hunters." For the well-intentioned, procrastinating is an art form.

Words alone won't get the job done, and neither will good intentions. Action is needed. Besides, we all know what the road to hell is paved with.

~ ~

A pompous, self-righteous politician dies. When he arrives up there, he knocks at the pearly gates. Saint Peter, appearing in his splendor of brilliance, answers the call. Glancing at the man and eager to know why he is there, Saint Peter asks, *"What is it you want?"*

Indignantly, the man responds, "I *want to come in."*

Amazed, Saint Peter questions, *"Oh! Why is that?"*

In exhilaration, the man replies, *"It's so peaceful here, no violence, happy children everywhere."*

"Yes." Saint Peter agrees with the politician's assessment and adds, *"We are aware and appreciative of our children. We work at taking care of them and each other. What have you done about the gun violence that is affecting the earth's children?"*

He dismisses Saint Peter's implication, pleading, *"Well, you see it's like this. I've been busy with my family, and a politician's work is so demanding. You know how that is. Time just slipped away, and before I knew it, I was here. But be assured, I always had plenty of good intentions."*

Softly smiling, Saint Peter replies, *"Ah! You are looking for the other place. The road there is paved with good intentions."*

~ ~

Be aware that the contradiction is that the very act of gun reform being challenged is your most potent weapon against your adversaries. It is the love that you express toward those who would do you harm during the direst circumstances that may bear fruit. Those who belittle you live in the shadow of their own smallness. Realizing your caring nature and expressing it is the elixir that may turn a heart of steel to pure gold, gold that softens hearts and change minds.

Seven

CHOICES *and* DECISIONS
Selection and Carry Through

The choices and decisions, including the choice of gun reform and the decision to fight for them, influence your lives direction. There is no greater assistance on your journey of change than the choices selected and decisions made. However, there is a very fine line between choices and decisions. You select a choice; you make a decision based on your selected choice.

Choices are two or more inner or outer appearances rising in your consciousness from which you select a preference. When you have selected a preference, it is a choice. What to do with, or about, the choice you have selected is your decision.

For example, a simple choice would be as follows: You are asked after dinner, "Would you prefer ice cream or pie for dessert?" You may think for a moment, but you don't have to concentrate intensely to select a choice. A simple choice doesn't require concentrated energy effort. Eating the entire dessert, or part of it is the decision you will make from the choice you have selected.

That is a simple example of choices and decisions. On your journey for gun reform, your choices and decisions may be more major than simple. A simple or difficult choice determines the decision and the amount of energy (concentrated energy) required to accomplish it. The simple or difficult choices and decisions are differentiated by the intensity of the rising energy invested and the interested attraction. Each may attract your attention, and the intensity of rising energy invested may increase or decrease, depending on many factors.

Once a choice is selected, the decision to do it kicks in. As you continue your journey for gun reform, you are constantly selecting from choices and making decisions. The rule of thumb is to select the choices that lead to the *necessary* decisions. It is the necessary decisions you make that help guide your progress.

There are no right or wrong decisions. There is only what is necessary. Therefore, you make your decisions based on what is needed at the moment or what is necessary for your journey, for gun reform, and in consideration of the need of others.

When a difficult decision must be made, the question is not "Is this right or wrong?" but "Is this necessary?" The right or wrong of any decision-making can only confuse and may cause problems. It is impossible, at the moment, to judge the right or wrong of any given situation.

Circumstances may change the right or wrong in any situation. What may be right today may be wrong tomorrow. Do what is necessary for the "now" and regrets will not manifest. Each momentary decision made is a momentary dedication, and when each is an essential decision, it becomes a steady, resolved dedication to your cause. Choices and decisions should be considered possibilities or opportunities allowing you to progress more swiftly toward your goal for gun reform. You should think carefully and wisely about the choices presented. A wise choice may allow you to make the necessary decision.

Choices and decisions are the signposts that point the way, a map that shows the necessary way to take you where you want to go. Each choice and decision takes you nearer to or further from the intended results. In your journey for gun reform, choices and decisions are constant occurrences. By the very nature of your chosen dedication to gun reform, choices and decisions arise.

As you continue your journey for gun reform, becoming aware of your Spiritual Heart Center (Chapter 13) and practicing the Minute Meditation (chapter 14) becomes an asset in selecting a choice and making the necessary decision. And, oh yes, you will have many options to choose from and many decisions to make. The journey that you are on will require it.

Eight

EMOTIONS
Rising Energy

On this courageous journey for gun reform, you will encounter many emotions: yours and those who confront you. It would be difficult for various emotions not to rise when you engage individuals who strongly oppose your views. Yet, your hearts are loving and kind. Therefore, it would be natural for emotions to rise when dealing with gun reform issues.

An emotion may be so quick to rise it may go unnoticed. Before you are aware, you may be caught up in it. This list of emotions may help you to identify and work with them.

Emotions rise in no particular order. They rise according to an individual's conditioning, disposition, personal history, experiences, or expectations. Reviewing a few of the various emotions may help you be aware of them. Awareness may give you the power to maintain an alert mind to handle emotions beneficially.

Anger

Anger is an emotion experienced as hostile feelings. Anger is not a bad or good emotion. It is an emotion that can be put to good use. The anger emotion will rise whenever a need for it exists, but it does not have to cause heartburn, figuratively or literally. To use anger constructively has enormous potential and power to right a wrong or correct an injustice.

You never want to repress anger. Allow yourself to experience it in a safe, productive way. Admit, "I am angry about such and such or so and so. I am so angry I could scream." If you are someplace where you can scream, do it. If not, take a few long deep breaths and use the Hand-To-Heart Exercise (chapter 15). Then when you are able – and choose to – decide the necessary action. Notice the emotion as it rises. Decide how best to express it.

You are not a doormat. Take whatever action is necessary to protect yourselves from those who would do you harm. Do not respond to the anger of others (including yourselves for getting angry). This only serves to compound it. Act from a loving heart no matter what action/s you take.

Your intention within the action is what matters. The appearance of anger may be negative, but the purpose of its expression need not be. Anger may contain the seeds of love. That is what dissipates anger and allows you to move on productively. For example, a teenager has wrecked the car. The parents are angry and prescribe punishment; however, within the prescribed punishment is their complete forgiveness, and they are thankful to God that no one was hurt. They can move on – and so can their child – without harboring ill will. The best blessing from your work with anger is that as the Minute Meditation practice dissipates anger, you may realize the freedom from letting go of the anger. It is a bonus: two for one, forgiveness and freedom.

2. *Excitement*

Excitement is a temporary stirring emotion. It can take you as quickly to the lows as the highs. There may be exciting moments as you progress on your journey. Yes, it is exciting to taste the fruits of your hard work. These times may be difficult, but wondrous adventures manifest in your daily lives.

Moments of excitement are natural, but when the moments are prolonged, the necessary judgment, reason, or common-sense decisions are temporarily stifled. So allow even the most exciting moments to pass quickly. Highs and lows are not sustainable. What goes up must come down!

Excitement may also contain an element of joy. Joy is the one emotion that the mind revels in; consequently, many opportunities for mischief abound. However, in time, you may transform the excitement emotion with joy to one of sobering contentment. It is better to be content.

3. *Fright*
Fright is an anxious moment when you dread moving toward an individual or situation. As you grow strong in your gun reform resolve, you may dare to meet others and do

the things you never expected. A little fright may serve a valuable purpose. A little stage fright does not prevent you from moving forward. It may even help you do what is necessary. There may always be a tinge of fright as you progress. It may help to keep the ego from overstepping *its* bounds.

4. *Frustration*

Frustration rises as irritating emotional energy. It usually rises when you experience a drought in your life or when you are prevented from doing something you want to do. In addition, the distractions of this world can cause it to be difficult for you to maintain a peaceful calm in your lives. Thus, frustrations begin.

Your perseverance and sincerity with your goal may overcome any frustration. Do not dialogue with the frustrating emotional disturbances. During the most frustrating times, you may become aware of that place of inner peace with patience and kindness.

If frustration is causing tears to flow, allow them; crying is purifying. Be gentle and especially loving with yourselves. A yearning, aching heart for your lost friends will move you inward and return you to inner calm.

5. *Grief*

You all are going through gut-wrenching emotional grief. Grief will rise to penetrate your heart and torment your lives. It may rise to fill a temporary vacuum that loss created. Your attachment to grief causes suffering and keeps you from moving beyond it. Grief is yours to do with as you wish.

Grief is no respecter of individual expressions of consciousness. It stalks all. Grief can hold you intently focused on your perceived loss. This may produce sporadic involuntary tearing and crying. Accept, allow, and respect grief's relative comings and goings.

No one can enter your space of rising, sorrowful, emotional intensity, no matter how sympathetic they are. Grief may not easily pass. It may cling for a time, then subside and fade in the background, only to rise again at intervals. Stained with your heartfelt memories, grief may repeatedly rise to trigger a reminder of your loss.

The Minute Meditation practice (chapter 14) allows you to experience your grief with a positive love for yourselves. You are taught to be aware of its rising and its falling. It's coming and going. You accept it for what it is – a rising emotion – then let it go by returning to the awareness of your Spiritual Heart Center *area* (chapter 13).

You may exorcize your grief outside meditation practice by noting the rising emotion, intensity, and sorrow that overshadows your heart. Only dialoging with an attachment to the rising grief can hold you, prisoner. Joy and grief exist in this world of opposites. Because within any opposite is its opposing force, the memories may be transformed from sorrowful grief to loving joy. It may occur when you are willing to express sincere gratitude for the time spent, love received, and life shared with the one/s you have lost.

In gratitude, a loss may become a gain. You are the recipient of all the love expressed, an heir to all that has gone before. You may release your loved one not to a grave but rather to the awareness of your Spiritual Heart Center. A loving relationship is a gift that remains with the giver and receiver. It is an expression of your being.

Rejoice that you were chosen to share love and companionship. Celebrate the passing as you did the coming. You can convert your tears of sorrow to tears of joy by realizing that which touched your heart *is* your heart.

6. *Hope*

Hope is a powerful force that freshens the internal wellspring of your lives. It softens each step of your inner walk. Hope picks you up after a fall and holds your hand as you continue your inner walk.

When your faith has temporarily withered, hope is what allows you to continue your journey for gun reform. Hope carries you through the mysterious shadows of doubts and dark nights of the soul. It permits you to get over, around, or through the obstacles on your path. Hope keeps you strong enough to take the next step *and* the next step.

7. *Humor*

Humor is an emotion that allows you to appreciate the comical in stressful situations. It may lighten a serious situation. Humor is one of the best relaxers and may improve your health.

Maintaining a sense of humor is essential. In times of sadness, learn to laugh at the apparent foolishness of this world. It may keep you from getting caught up in frustrations. Your chosen journey is difficult enough, but it is next to impossible without an appreciation for the comical.

8. *Love*

You will find as many definitions of love as there are individuals who express it one moment and withdraw it the next. Precisely because love can turn on a dime, it isn't easy to define. Poets write about one sort of love.

Romance novels are full of it. You can use and misuse love and yet seldom understand it. You may withhold it as though it were a coin in your pocket to spend whenever you please. Coins are useless unless you spend them. Love is worthless unless you express it.

Love may bask in the sun's rays or hide in the shadow of the night. Love is a force to be reckoned with when used for good or ill. The question may arise: Is there an *if*? "I will love you *if* you love me." That is called commercial love. Commercial love, laden with all the *ifs,* is mired in a slush of emotional attachments and costs.

The list of ifs is endless." I will love you *if* you stay, *if* you do as I say *if* you will change, *if* you put up with my abuse, *if* you never disagree with me, etc. You may have more "ifs" to add to the list. This world is replete with love's ifs, and they may come in multiple disguises.

The Listening-in exercise (chapter 15) may deepen your hearing ability and help you be aware of the "ifs" and realize that unconditional love is beyond all of the ifs. Unconditional love does not include ifs. It is aware of its Beloved, you, and embraces you under all circumstances.

9. *Regret*

Regret rises with a mistaken thought, word, or deed against yourselves or others. Regret has a mesmerizing effect on your mind's memory. It holds you in the past that no longer exists. It pains your heart, twists your mind, and holds you in a time warp.

Regret requires your full attention. It will torment you into believing you should have or could have done something differently. When you accept the responsibility for harming yourselves or others, you turn away from the misconduct. You may even make amends. However, constantly revisiting the regret is like constantly replaying a broken record. It causes the needle (you) to get caught in a groove.

Wallowing in regretful sorrow is not productive or necessary. You treat it the same way you treat guilt: you notice it, do not deny it, do not dialogue with it, and let it go. This gives you the freedom to bathe in unconditional love.

10. *Rejection*

There may be a time when rejection by others is overwhelming, and your hearts will ache for relief. Using the No-Power Exercise (chapter 15 and the Minute Meditation chapter 14) is your greatest protection from abuse, rudeness, or insults. You may understand that the abuse by others is their problem, not yours. Those who would reject you and heap rudeness upon you do harm to themselves. Hold your heads high, lead with your hearts, and be aware that your best efforts, at times, will not be enough. You are not held accountable for the rejection by others. With the help of the Minute Meditation practice, you may develop the ability to handle rejection. You are then free to live the lives you have chosen.

~ ~

Emotions do have a value determined by their circumstances. Repressing an emotion may be as detrimental to you as overexpressing it. The Minute Meditation practice may neutralize and balance the rising emotions by teaching you to neither repress nor deny them. In time, with practice, you may no longer be under the domination of any emotion.

The intensity of any emotion expressed is the result of complex conditioning. However, that intensity is subject to your modification. A contented life requires that all phases of your life are emotionally balanced. As you are aware of the emotions as they rise, you may establish the necessary balance.

Notice how emotions may affect you and the difference they can make in your daily life. It is advantageous to be aware of the emotions as they rise. However, you need never be held captive by any emotion. It is your choice!

NINE

ACCEPT, ALLOW
and
RESPECT
An Atmosphere of Peace

Accepting, allowing, and respecting expresses reverence for all human beings. On your journey for gun reform, you will meet individuals on the same journey, on different journeys, and those who are just sleepwalking through life. There is always the temptation to judge where you are on your journey and where others may be; this is a trap easily stepped into. To accept, allow, and respect yourselves and others gives you the freedom of movement among the many.

Accept, allow, and respect may bring to your journey an atmosphere of peace. Your journey for gun reform is proof of your accepting, allowing, and respecting all individuals. There is no greater proof than placing yourselves out there to save lives.

There are benefits received and given when you can accept, allow, and respect the differences presented by individuals from all walks of life. Change is possible when you allow others to express themselves in an atmosphere of peaceful exchange. You have shown the ability to do that.

Giving the respect, you believe you deserve contributes to a positive state of mind. Respect for yourselves and others may bring awareness of the humanity in others. Accepting, allowing, and respecting all individual points of view does not mean you are less firm, forceful, and progressive on your journey for gun reform. On the contrary, you may find that you are stronger, firmer, and more progressive when you accept, allow, and respect the most negative among you.

~ ~

Your journey for gun reform is the most difficult one, but you are blessed with youth *and* guts to accomplish the necessary changes. Your staying power will be in your belief in a worthy cause *and* each other. You have been blessed with the glue that holds you together – love. And you all have demonstrated an abundance of it. Your challengers claim to need their guns to protect themselves and save lives. You are using your hearts to do the same. Yours is the better choice.

Ten

DEDICATION
Discouraged and Tested

Yes, on your dedicated journey for gun reform, you can count on being discouraged and tested. But beware that discouragement clouds the mind and creates obstacles that do not exist. There will be times when discouragement will raise its ugly head. When your journey becomes difficult, discouragement may sap your energy and shake your dedication to gun reform.

Discouragement has a way of giving you leave to abandon your goal at the time it is most needed. Discouragement opens the door to those who would foster events or situations that would allow you to become discouraged with your dedication. Your journey is not dependent on anyone's opinion or negativity. It is yours to protect against the naysayers who would take you toward discouragement. Discouragement will rise according to circumstances; as with all circumstances, they change.

When discouragement's shadow nears, your best defense is to renew your dedication—always remembering your fallen friends and the price they paid. There will always be those among you who will ridicule and challenge your dedication. Your dedication honors those to whom you are devoted.

Throughout all of the ups and downs, your dedication allows you to push past the drama, complaints, and criticism. When the odds are against you during dark times, your dedication refuses to give up and forges ahead. When you are worn, tired, and disturbed by disappointments, your dedication reminds you of your purpose. Dedication is one-pointed and eventually penetrates the most discouraging of appearances.

There is no doubt that there will be times when your journey for gun reform will feel like a trial by fire. You may be tested for what you believe is beyond your limits. Yet, during these times, you must renew your dedication and remind yourselves that yours is a worthy cause beyond any limit that this world could place upon it.

Whenever you are tested, it is with selfless dedication that you can overcome the challenges and difficulties you may encounter. Sometimes, you will be tempted to succumb to the belief that you are being tested beyond your strength and feel the agony of being tested. During these times, you must be aware that whenever your light is at its brightest, the darkness will rise in the form of a friend or foe to dismantle you into a billion parts.

You are never beyond the vicious attacks from those who cannot bask in your light. For them, their pain is real. Their discomfort is a torment. They rise to test you in their abject misery. Is it any wonder that you are their target? You dare to challenge them. Whenever you are tempted to believe you are tested beyond your limits, have faith and never doubt that you do possess the inner strength to withstand any outer verbal attacks against you. You are in the most Blessed state of Grace when being tested. Dedication puts a paintbrush in your hands and guides every stroke upon the canvas until the most beautiful appears.

ELEVEN

HUGS
God's Embrace

Allow me to share my favorite activity, hugs. Hugs are a gift of an acceptance greeting or parting embrace. A gentle hug usually abounds among friends. Anyone watching the "March For Our Lives" could easily observe the abundance of hugs among the thousands of protesters, the youth, the speakers, and the teenage organizers. There was no lack of hugs. There was plenty to go around.

There is a tendency to hug those with whom you feel comfortable or who may have kind intentions toward you. All of this is well and good. Hugs are underappreciated in all they may accomplish among your brothers and sisters on this earth plane. However, to restrict or limit hugs to a particular group of individuals is to restrict or limit your infinite nature of giving.

Hugs should not be given as an afterthought or off-the-cuff gesture. They should be thoughtful, caring, gentle, and given without a desire for compensation (i.e., if you share a hug, you may be liked better). That is not a caring hug. That is a commercial hug.

A hug isn't just a feel-good expression of warmth. It is a nonverbal communication that allows the vibrating energy of either or both recipients to express without words a heartfelt caring through the sense of touch. Hugs will enable you to share your calm, vibrating energy, the energy that may bring calm where there is disruption, depression, or fear. A gentle hug's greatest benefit is that you cannot give a hug without simultaneously receiving one.

Hugs are the visible proof of the spiritual principle: in giving, you receive. An appropriate gentle hug may allow you to express your uncompromising loving nature. Hugs may provide comfort, joy, and, when most needed, an emotional lift.

When you are presented with an opportunity to hug another whom you do not know well, and you do reach out in a non-threatening, gentle, and caring embrace, the blessings *you* may receive are manifold.

Hugs have a rescuing power. Within a gentle hug's endearing embrace, you and your family of soldier civilians may find the strongest sustaining power on your journey for gun reform.

Because of the inherent power in every sincere hug, healing of mind, emotions, or body may occur. If you are ever seeking the experience of the embrace of God, be aware that God's embrace is yours. The only way you may experience God's embrace on this earth is for you to embrace another. You are the heart, arms, and hands of God. You can gently hug the God of others as the God of yourself.

TWELVE

TOPIC
TIPS
Practical Guidance

The Topic Tips are written to support and guide you on your journey to bring about gun reform. In your day-to-day life experiences, the topic tips may allow you to understand the outer and inner world quickly. Enjoy them!

Topic Tips:

1. You are a worthy being with certain gifts. Express them!

2. You are constantly living at the beginning, not an end.

3. Guilt is a tormentor that rubs salt in an open wound. Guilt never cured an illness or solved a problem.

4. There are many opportunities for mischief. However, the Minute Meditation may transform exciting emotions into sobering contentment.

5. Inner joy rests in peace beyond understanding. It's a quiet, gentle inner joy that sees you through the sadness of worldly

events. Once you have experienced this inner joy, it adds color to your outer world. To lose it would be to return to a black-and-white world.

6. No need to get upset with what is going on with your work to make gun reform. Renew your priority and continue your journey. You are not starting over, beginning again, or going backward. You are continuing.

7. A proactive lifestyle may require flexibility at any time. Go with what you have, wherever you are.

8. Think twice before you speak, three times before you act because what you send out by thought or the spoken word will surely, "return to the sender."

9. The beauty of mistakes is that they are never an end but a beginning. They allow for starting over.

10. Fortunately, attitudes and emotional states are not set in concrete. Change

is possible when you are persistent and dedicated to making it happen.

11. You can handle rejection. You are free to live the good life. Vibrating energy is vibrating energy. Any negative vibrating energy may be transformed.

12. There is deep emotional pleasure in the fruits of the Minute Meditation practice. Less stress, more patience, and a gentle connection to your Spiritual Heart Center *area* are but a few of the fruits.

THIRTEEN

YOUR SPIRITUAL HEART CENTER
Pure Energy

As promised, here is a review of your Spiritual Heart Center, The Minute Meditation, and The Minute Meditation practice. They may help you overcome difficult times during your journey for gun reform. Balance and a firm dedication may be provided with the least effort.

A profound, subtle vibrating energy exists within your physical form at the center of your chest, between the breasts. It is not an object or feeling you can experience. It is referred to as the Spiritual Heart Center, your other heart, and in the East, as the 4th Chakra. An old story goes like this: after God created humankind, God called one of God's angels and asked the angel to hide the one thing God wished to conceal.

"I have finished except for one thing, the mystery of life. Where shall you hide it?" God asked the angel.

"I will hide it in outer space," responded the excited angel.

"No," said God, *"someone will easily find it there one day."*

"All right, I will hide it on the moon. Surely, it will not be found there?"

"No, no," said God, *"one day they will be able to look there also. Mmm,"* thought God, *"I have it! Put it within them. They would never think to look there."*

Your Spiritual Heart Center is right at your fingertips. Every time you touch the center of your chest area, you point to your Spiritual Heart Center. You need look no further. You have found it.

You may realize the Spiritual Heart Center, the innermost sacred place of your being. It is your Holy of Holies. The Minute Meditation is the revelation that reveals where and how you may access your Spiritual Heart Center.

FOURTEEN

THE MINUTE MEDITATION PRACTICE

The Minute Meditation may take you straight to your Spiritual Heart Center, "your other heart," and your inner power source. There is no extraneous dialogue and no stringent guidelines. There are no hindrances of any kind between you and your inner source.

The Minute Meditation is for you who have an interest in the present "now" without mental or verbal words, in solitude, simplicity, and silence. A word, verbally or mentally, is *not* necessary. It is a silent meditation practice that may open your Spiritual Heart Center and allow you to keep a necessary balance on your journey for gun reform.

Start your silent meditation practice with one minute twice daily, allowing the practice time to extend naturally. Be consistent. Practice twice a day. If, for any reason, you find it difficult to become aware of the Spiritual Heart Center area, place your hand on your Spiritual Heart Center *area* for the first few Minute Meditation practices.

The Practice

1. Sit comfortably on a chair or couch. If you prefer, sit on a cushion on the floor. Close your eyes, and rest your hands gently on your lap or by your sides.

2. Slowly inhale deeply and slowly exhale, relaxing your entire body. Consciously, become aware of your Spiritual Heart Center *area* (center of the chest, between the breasts) and rest with awareness of this *area*. Continue to breathe normally.

3. If thoughts or sensations rise, do not dialogue, converse, engage, or respond to their rising (your attention is already there). Allow them to rise and again gently become aware of your Spiritual Heart Center *area*.

~ ~

Is this easy enough? Continue the practice in this manner. No matter how often thoughts, emotions, or any of the senses rise, gently again become aware of your Spiritual Heart Center **area**. You are not to focus on feeling the Spiritual Heart Center nor attempt to rest or still the mind.

There is nothing to feel. It is just awareness of the Spiritual Heart Center *area*. In doing so, the mind rests each time you return to rest with awareness of your Spiritual Heart Center *area*. Do *not* label any of the rising thoughts, emotions, or senses. For example, a bird singing, all that is occurring is the sense of hearing rising. The identity "bird" is a conditioning label, don't use it.

At the end of your silent meditation practice period, take a few moments to become aware of your mental and physical senses before returning to normal activities. Practice the Minute Meditation at any time before a meal, at least two hours after a meal, and about an hour after liquid juices (the changing energy vibration will interfere with the digestion process). Water is fine.

The Minute Meditation may awaken you to the entrance door of your inner life. It may bring you to the realization of the present and a life lived in the present. When you can be in the present, the hurts, sufferings, and emotional pain of this world may be healed.

Be patient with your practice. There is no hurry. Allow the process to give rest to a restless mind. Accept there is no one rushing you. Trust the bumps on the path will smooth out as you wear them down. Every moment you practice may help to smooth out a rough spot.

All too often, you may become attached to a particular time, place, or sitting cushion. You want everything to be the same—nothing out of order. In most situations, that would be ideal. But with the Minute Meditation, the ideal is not necessary. You must be flexible enough to adjust to a moment of change as it presents itself.

Your days may be long and busy. Work, school, and dedication to gun reform can occupy your days and evenings. You may believe there is no time for a meditation practice, but not with the Minute Meditation. You go to the John sometime during your busy day. Well, stay on the John for a minute more. John may become your best friend.

Be flexible. Flexibility gives you the freedom to adjust, correct, reconsider and change. Once your time and place are established, making even a temporary change may be resisted. An active lifestyle may require flexibility at any time. Be prepared to adjust to new surroundings and accept the changes as they may occur.

Being flexible will allow you to adapt your practice whenever and wherever necessary. If you are not flexible, traveling for a time to a strange environment could cause an interruption of your practice. Do not trouble yourselves with the outer appearances of change in your life.

You are never locked into a rigid position. Inner and outer growth causes changes and requires flexibility for you to adjust and accept changes as they may occur. Time is relative to this plane of opposites. When you begin a silent meditation practice, you start with a minute twice daily. It is not necessary to intentionally place strict time limits on your silent practice. Allow your practice to expand itself. This allows your mind and body to adjust naturally.

You do not want to judge your practice periods by length. Longer is not better, nor is shorter worse. The important issue is to do the practice twice a day. One minute is an eternity in the silence of awareness.

Your practice will eventually become a habit. The time necessary for your practice will become established and comfortable. There never is a need to force your practice time. If you are restless or uncomfortable, get up and return to the practice at another time when you are at ease.

The fruit of your practice may be experienced on your journey for gun reform and as you respond to the needs of others and your own legitimate needs. A silent meditation practice need not be dreaded, nor should it be forced. Time, place, cushions, and shawls may be helpful tools, but all you ever need to practice the Minute Meditation is you. Your practice will meet your need in its own time. Relax and let the practice do you.

FIFTEEN

MINI-EXERCISES
Helpers

The mini-exercises are offered as helpers. Using them may bring solace and calm as you progress on your journey for gun reform. Use them when needed.

NO-POWER EXERCISE

The No-Power Exercise is an exercise that may allow you to address a particularly thorny issue that comes up repeatedly at various times. It is its own unique exercise and is to be used *only* when necessary. Its sole purpose is to remove invested power in an internal sense-impression (a specific tormenting issue of thought, word, or deed that has made a tormenting impression in your consciousness).

The No-Power Exercise does not replace your twice-daily silent Minute Meditation practice. And the exercise is never to be mixed during the Minute Meditation practice. The internal sense-impression may be experienced as a solid steel form — non-penetrable. It may be the most difficult vibrating energy to **remove your power from**. Because you have given it power by previously accepting a false belief in it, attempting to make the slightest dent may be a constant struggle.

The power is directly given to you from within, and you are the one who invests or withholds the power. An internal sense-impression of itself cannot attach. You attach, detach, give it life and death, and you may shed the false image of the impression. You learn to forgive yourself and those who may have done you harm. The "No Power Exercise" may bring you into a neutral zone of non-responding and restore your inner peace, an integral part of the exercise.

You *never* use the No-Power exercise while driving or operating any mechanical equipment. In addition, you do not use the No-Power Exercise whenever your safety is at risk. No meditation or mini-exercise should be used during these times.

This is not a "no" dialogue practice like The Minute Meditation practice is. When you use "*No-Power God is,*" you are using a specifically targeted dialogue exercise. There is no mixing of the No-Power Exercise while doing The Minute Meditation practice. The major difference between a *"no"* dialogue practice (The Minute Meditation) and a targeted dialogue exercise (No-Power Exercise) is its use for the result of taking back your invested power from a particular impression that would not respond during the ordinary scheme of things.

The Exercise:
A. When a tormenting thought arises during your daily activities, silently repeat, *"No- Power, God Is,"* as often as is necessary.

B. Immediately refocus your attention on the outer activity.

When using the no-power exercise, it is most important to remember the immediacy of responding, ***"No-Power, God Is."*** The *"No-Power"* is your realization that the tormenting thought of itself has no power. The **"*GOD IS*"** acknowledges that only God is, and God alone exists right there in the moment of the tormenting thoughts rising.

2. THE HAND-TO-HEART EXERCISE
A Quick Temporary Solution

Standing up for change may create times of highs and lows. At times your energy may vibrate at such a rapid speed that you may feel like you are on a roller coaster. Whenever you are an instrument of change, there may be resistance to change; and an inner or outer struggle may occur.

If immediate help is unavailable, the silent Hand-to-Heart Exercise may be a short-term solution. This exercise may be used anywhere and during any activity except when your safety is at risk. The silent Hand-to-Heart Exercise may help bring immediate calm and may restore your vibrating energy's balance.

The Exercise
A. When your inner vibrating energy turmoil besieges you, rest your hand on the area of your Spiritual Heart Center (center of the chest between the breasts).

B. Take a long deep breath, exhale slowly while relaxing your mind and body. Rest your attention on your hand (not on the awareness of your Spiritual Heart Center) in the silence of awareness. If necessary, repeat several times.

Do not be fooled by the simplicity of this mini-exercise. Hands are many times used to heal or to bless. The Hand-to-Heart Exercise is empowered with the essence of your inner power.

3. THE LISTENING-IN EXERCISE
The Inner Silence

The Listening-In Exercise is the inner ability to hear the silent, non-verbal voice of your inner guidance. As you rest in your Spiritual Heart Center area, the ability to turn a "listening-in" ear to hear may increase. In the silence of your Spiritual Heart Center, the openness and emptiness are rooted in the bedrock of your inner power's abiding presence. The inner silence may become so deafening that it is loud and clear.

The Exercise

A. Whenever you have a situation, condition, or question that you feel a need for help from your inner guidance, you may sit quietly with your eyes open or closed.

B. Place your awareness on your Spiritual Heart Center area. Then, softly, listen-in to the inner silence. Listen as though you were waiting for a phone to ring.

~ ~

Over time with the practice of listening-to the inner silence within your Spiritual Heart Center, you may find a silent, sacred language that speaks to you without words. As you progress on your journey of changes, your understanding and insights may deepen. When you are prepared and ready to receive, there is nothing that you are denied.

SIXTEEN

MAINTENANCE
And
BALANCE
A Strong, Positive Presence

You have the essential hearts and guts for what it takes to wake up a sleeping nation. Your goal is within reach if you can maintain a balance and continue with a strong-sounding, positive presence. It may be the most difficult journey to travel, yet it may be a joyous one. Do not hesitate to continue your journey with gun reform. Keep a balance when under pressure.

Yes, you need to handle the outer daily activities attentively and responsibly. You can do all things well in the service of your loving hearts without getting a grade. The intimidating mind of judging may pop up when you are grading yourselves or expecting others to grade you. Give it up.

You may not always see the immediate results of your exhausting efforts before you. Planting seeds for change may require time. There may not be instant gratification. So be patient and persistent, and keep your eyes on the light (you) that penetrates the darkness. Yes, there will be the "naysayers." There will be attempts to separate you by race, ethnicity, gender, age, and sexual choice. An effort to turn you against each other and divide and conquer is in full swing.

The opposition may believe, given time and separation (college, work), your numbers will decrease, and your voices will become a murmur. Realize there is always the opportunity to increase as you enter an expanded Universe. Your chosen journey cannot be left behind, because it is in your heart and, therefore, may be taken with you anywhere you find yourselves. Guts infused with love are a powerful force.

Practice the Minute Meditation and keep a sense of humor when teeter-tottering. So, trip, scrape your knees, tire, be tempted, doubt, struggle, cry, and complain. It matters naught if it is not fun. Remember that you are the chosen ones who can get the job done.

AUTHOR

Carla R. Mancari is an author of many books, a life guide, a teacher, and a leader of retreats to improve individuals' (from all walks of life) self-confidence, self-esteem, and teach them how to meet life's challenges. For more than 45 years, she has guided individuals in understanding life's spiritual principles, spiritual activities, and rising emotions in their private and daily lives. Her greatest joy is helping individuals to realize their self-worth, unique gifts/talents, full potential, *and* to wake up to their spirituality.

Carla is the recipient of The Christ Centered Prayer Meditation revelation, The Minute Meditation, and The Heart-Centered Meditation Practice. She is a co-founder of the Contemplative Invitation Teaching. Although Carla had never attended high school and was labeled a retarded child, she attained two University degrees: a B.A. from the University of South Carolina in Columbia, South Carolina, and an MEd from South Carolina State University in Orangeburg,

South Carolina. Carla studied at Brigham Young University and attended the School of the Americas in Switzerland.

Carla led a class-action suit in the United States Supreme Court to protect minorities' rights (Morton vs. Mancari, 1973) and was a certified psychologist. She served in the United States Air Force. Traveling worldwide for many years, Carla studied with Christian, Hindu, and Buddhist masters. She was a guest on the Larry King Show, and a guest lecturer at various colleges, professional groups, and book signings.

Carla gained national recognition when featured in *Good Housekeeping*, "The Education of Carla Mancari, 1969." It chronicled her life in 1967-68 when she was the first white student to receive a Master's degree from the then all-Black South Carolina State College in Orangeburg, South Carolina.

Author's Books

Mancari, Carla R., *When Jesus Is the Guru: A Wayward Christian's Spiritual Walk.* Celestial Literary Group, 2010.

- - - *Eco-You: A Power of One, Improve Your Health, Improve Your Life.* Celestial Literary Group, 2019.

- - - *Walking on the Grass: A White Woman In A Black World.* Celestial Literary Group, 2016.

- - - *The 4th Chakra: Your Spiritual Heart Center – How to Quickly Access It.* Celestial Literary Group, 2016.

- - - *Abortion and The Bible: The Abortion Dilemma: A Scriptural Response, A Woman's Spirituality.* Celestial Literary Group, 2017.

- - - *Racism: The Pain of Invisibility.* Celestial Literary Group, 2017.

- - - *The Rising Emotions: Understanding and Mastering Them.* Celestial Literary Group, 2017.

- - - *The Mystical Path: The Serious Student.* Celestial Literary Group, 2017.

- - - *Spiritual Principles: Understanding, Realizing, and Living Them.* Celestial Literary Group, 2018.

- - - *Climate Change: Consciousness Change.* Celestial Literary Group, 2017.

- - - *Words: Locks On The Door or Keys To The Kingdom.* Celestial Literary Group, 2018.

- - - *Aging: Physical to the Mystical.* Celestial Literary Group, 2018.

- - - *Divine Love: Your Nature.* Celestial Literary Group, 2018.

- - - *The Lazarus Rising: The Kundalini – A Rising Dormant Energy.* Celestial Literary Group, 2018.

\- - - *Depression: Hopelessness.* Celestial Literary Group, 2018.

\- - - *Jesus Christ: Teacher.* Celestial Literary Group, 2018.

\- - - *The Transformation: Change of Heart.* Celestial Literary Group, 2018.

\- - - *The Mystical Surrender: Giving In.* Celestial Literary Group, 2018.

\- - - *Death Ain't Dead: Empty Graves.* Celestial Literary Group, 2018.

\- - - *Common Decency: Your DNA.* Celestial Literary Group, 2018.

\- - - *Christians?: Common Decency.* Celestial Literary Group, 2018.

\- - - *Beyond Buddhism: Meditations.* Celestial Literary Group, 2018.

\- - - *Exit: Get Ready, Set, Go.* Celestial Literary Group, 2018.

- - - *Meditation: Good For You*. Celestial Literary Group, 2018.

- - - *How To Love "You:" Begins with You*. Celestial Literary Group, 2018.

- - - *Consciousness: Yours*. Celestial Literary Group, 2018.

- - - *Suicide: Understanding It*. Celestial Literary Group, 2018.

- - - *Detachment: Realizations*. Celestial Literary Group, 2018.

- - - *Detachment: Christian*. Celestial Literary Group, 2018.

- - - *Sexual Abuse: By The Church – Its Root, Coerced Celibacy*. Celestial Literary Group, 2018.

- - - *Guns and Guts: The Courage To Act*. Celestial Literary Group, 2018.

- - - *Jesus, The Way: A Mystical Understanding.* Celestial Literary Group, 2019.

- - - *Motivation: Self-Motivated.* Celestial Literary Group, 2019.

- - - *Totally Free: Is Killing Me.* Celestial Literary, Group, 2018.

- - - *A 30-Second Meditation For Teenagers.* Celestial Literary Group, 2018.

- - - *A 30-Second Meditation For Seniors.* Celestial Literary Group, 2017.

- - - *The Five Faces Of Love.* Celestial Literary Group, 2019.

- - - *Angel In The House.* Celestial Literary Group, 2019 (A Children's book).

- - - *Put It In The Bible: Prayerful Requests,* Celestial Literary Group, 2019.

- - - *Loneliness: Heartache,* Celestial Literary Group, 2019.

- - - *Hate: A Dark Emotion,* Celestial Literary Group, 2019.

- - - *Greed: It's Addictive.* Celestial Literary Group, 2019.

- - - *On Being Young: Choices.* Celestial Literary Group, 2019.

- - - *Gratitude: Expressed, Sincere.* Celestial Literary Group, 2019.

- - - *Humor: A Necessity.* Celestial Literary Group, 2019.

- - - *A Christian: Are You One?* Celestial Literary Group, 2019.

- - - *A Habit: How To Switch Meditation Practices.* Celestial Literary Group, 2019.

- - - *Impeachment: Living On The Dark Side.* Celestial Literary Group, 2019.

- - - *The Jesus I Know.* Celestial Literary Group, 2019.

- - - *Grace: Spirit And Truth.* Celestial Literary Group, 2019.

- - - *Temptation.* Celestial Literary Group, 2019.

- - - *The Christian Journey: Teacher Student Relationship.* Celestial Literary Group, 2019.

- - - *The Beloved: Who Is The Beloved?* Celestial Literary Group, 2019.

- - - *What Now, Lord? Enlightenment.* Celestial Literary Group, 2019.

- - - *What If I Were Gay?* Celestial Literary Group, 2019.

- - - *Mother Mary: Mother of Jesus.* Celestial Literary Group, 2019.

- - - *I Remember America.* Celestial Literary Group, 2019.

- - - *The Overcoming: "Jesus."* Celestial Literary Group, 2019.

- - - *When Faith Is Not Enough.* Celestial Literary Group, 2019.

- - - *The Plane of Opposites: The Work.* Celestial Literary Group, 2020.

- - - *Crisis.* Celestial Literary Group, 2020.

- - - *Grief: Gut-Wrenching Emotion.* Celestial Literary Group, 2020.

- - - *God.* Celestial Literary Group, 2020.

- - - *Regrets: Do You Have Any?* Celestial Literary Group, 2020.

- - - *1968, 1968,1968: The Mind of A Racist.* Celestial Literary Group, 2020.

- - - *Satan.* Celestial Literary Group, 2020.

- - - *Practice Practice: Meditation.* Celestial Literary Group, 2021.

\- - - *Metaphysical Questions With Answers From The Spiritual Heart Center.* Celestial Literary Group, 2021.

\- - - *Christians Without Jesus: Prodigal Son's Journey.* Celestial Literary Group, 2021.

\- - - *From Here To There.* Celestial Literary Group, 2021.

\- - - *An Awakening Path: Christian Spiritual Principles.* Celestial Literary Group, 2021.

\- - - *Holy Scripture: Uplifting, Inspiring and Comforting.* Celestial Literary Group, 2021.

\- - - *Male Female: The Split Soul.* Celestial Literary Group, 2021.

\- - - *The Inner Message: Theological Mystical State.* Celestial Literary Group, 2021.

\- - - *A Guide To Understanding Mind's Contents And Realizations.* Celestial Literary Group, 2021.

- - - *A Sister's Laughter: Oh! How I Miss It!* Celestial Literary Group, 2021.

- - - *Churches: Are They Necessary?* Celestial Literary Group, 2021.

- - - *Metaphysical Stories and Poems.* Celestial Literary Group, 2021.

- - - *Jesus, Jesus, Jesus.* Celestial Literary Group, 2021.

- - - *The Disciple and The Mystical Guide.* Celestial Literary Group, 2021.

- - - *The Holy Trinity: 1+1+1=1, No Mystery.* Celestial Literary Group, 2021.

- - - *Fear of Jesus.* Celestial Literary Group, 2021.

- - - *Symbols and Rituals: Christian.* Celestial Literary Group, 2021.

- - - *Christian Minute Meditation.* Celestial Literary Group, 2021.

- - - *Christian Minute Meditation: Pocket Size.* Celestial Literary Group, 2021.

- - - *The Spiritual Heart Center: Pocket Size.* Celestial Literary Group, 2021.

- - - *The Spiritual Heart Center.* Celestial Literary Group, 2021.

- - - *Sin.* Celestial Literary Group, 2021.

- - - *Compassion.* Celestial Literary Group, 2021.

- - - *Silence.* Celestial Literary Group, 2021.

- - - *The Christ Centered Prayer Meditation Teaching Guide.* Celestial Literary Group, 2022.

- - - *Spiritual Zone.* Celestial Literary Group, 2022.

- - - *Bible Scriptures: Mystical Understanding.* Celestial Literary Group, 2022.

- - - *Lead Us Not.* Celestial Literary Group, 2022.

- - - *Let's Talk About Jesus, Or Not.* Celestial Literary Group, 2022.

- - - *For The Love of Jesus.* Celestial Literary Group, 2022.

- - - *Abortion, When Life Does Not Begin! Exodus 21:22-25.* Celestial Literary Group, 2022.

- - - *Morton vs. Mancari: A Plaintiff's Response: How An Average Joe (woman) Landed In The US Supreme Court.* Celestial Literary Group, 2022.

- - - *Christian Spiritual Exercises: The Inner Journey.* Celestial Literary Group, 2023.

Casey-Martus, Sandra, and Mancari, Carla R. *The Lessons, Volume One: How to Understand Spiritual Principles, Spiritual Activities, and Rising Emotions, 2nd Edition.* Celestial Literary Group, 2020.

\- - - *The Lessons Volume Two: How to Understand Spiritual Principles, Spiritual Activities, and Rising Emotions, 2nd Edition.* Celestial Literary Group, 2020.

\- - - *The Christ Centered Prayer: Revelation, Strait Gate and Narrow Way, Second Edition.* Celestial Literary Group, 2018

\- - - *Your Other Heart: The Best Kept Secret, Second Edition.* Celestial Literary Group, 2011.

\- - - *The Scripture Prayer: Praying The Scriptures.* Celestial Literary Group, 2020.

\- - - *The Christ Centered Prayer Meditation Practice: Pocket Size.* Celestial Literary Group, 2021.

Carpenter, Mary B., and Mancari, Carla R. *The Minute Meditation, Book 1: It Is Profound!* Celestial Literary Group, 2022.

\- - -*The Minute Meditation, Book 2: Workbook, (The Minute Meditation, It Is*

Profound!). The Celestial Literary Group, 2022.

- - - *The Minute Meditation, It Is Profound! Book 3: The Essentials.* Celestial Literary Group, 2022.

- - - *The Minute Meditation, It Is Profound! Book 4: A Diet For The Soul.* Celestial Literary Group, 2022.

- - - *The Minute Meditation, It Is Profound! Book 5: The Three of You, You Are Never Alone.* Celestial Literary Group, 2022.

- - - *The Minute Meditation, It Is Profound! Book 6: Pocket Size.* Celestial Literary Group, 2022.

- - - *The Minute Meditation, It Is Profound! Book 7 – Teaching Guide.* Celestial Literary Group, 2022.

- - - *A Scriptural Reference: For The Lessons: How to Understand Spiritual Principles, Spiritual Activities, and Rising*

Emotions, Volumes One and Two, 2ⁿᵈ Edition. Celestial Literary Group, 2020.

- - - *Spirituality: Yours.* Celestial Literary Group, 2021.

- - - *Dreams: States of Consciousness.* Celestial Literary Group, 2021.

Websites:
http://www.christcenteredprayerpractice.com/

~~

*You are Heaven and Earth
and all things in between.
You are a Moment now
seen and unseen.*

NOTES

www.ingramcontent.com/pod-product-compliance
Lightning Source LLC
Chambersburg PA
CBHW020442220526
45464CB00002B/817